Miles AND THE Grumpy Pants

Author
Zachary Locker

Illustrator
Sadiqa Akhter

Dedication

This book is dedicated to my son, Miles; along with his twin brothers, Everett and Preston; his sister, Roxie; and their mom and my beautiful wife, Brittany, without whom none of this 'almost' true story happens.

Copyright

Every morning Miles
wakes up and
must get dressed.
But he does not
like picking out his pants.

No matter what he does...barely cracking the door.

Or, sneaking in quietly with all the lights off.

Or, surprising his pants with his Ninja skills.

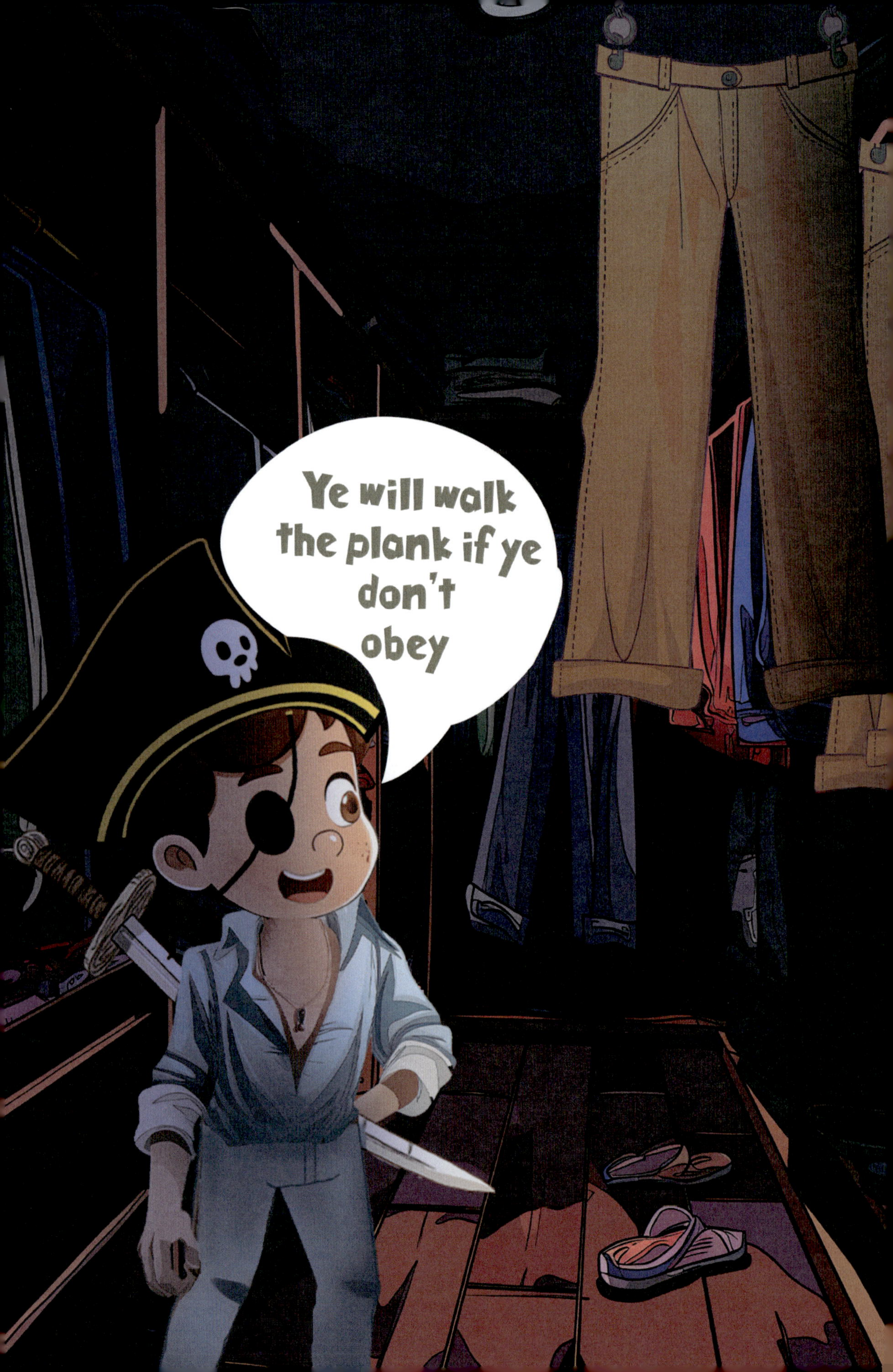
Ye will walk the plank if ye don't obey

Or, threatening them with
his best Pirate impression.

And,
even begging his
little sister for help.

He ALWAYS ends up
with Grumpy Pants.

So he heads downstairs for breakfast, but everything makes him grumpy.

There's way too much
milk in his cereal.

The butter melted too
fast on his pancakes.

Sometimes he wear his
grumpy pants all day long.
From the bus to recess to
the last class of the day,
Miles is just plain grumpy.

But other days, Mom
and Dad realize
what has happened.

So they spring into action!
Dad runs upstairs and
scolds the pants.

Meanwhile Mom wrestles the pants off Miles and puts them in the laundry for a thorough washing out.

After selecting a
pair of Perfectly Good
Pants, Mom, Dad,
and Miles celebrate!

Until Miles heads
out the door only
to realize that
these....are
Whiny Pants.

Made in the USA
Middletown, DE
30 May 2024